THE LAFFER

CURVE

The Laffer Curve relates increasing tax

rates to rising, then falling, tax revenues.

Its existence and values are crucial to a

measure of the limits on the ability for

particular countries to raise taxes – or even

survive and stay solvent.

BY

TIM WALSHAW

ISBN: 978-0-6487689-2-0

Previous related publication by Tim Walshaw:

Increasing Returns to Scale: A Simple Way to Make Good

Investments, and Not Bad Investments, When Investing in Company

Shares. Published 2014. Economic Rents, the Hidden Profit: How to Find

Safe Companies to Invest In. Published 2015. Double Entry Bookkeeping.

2018. Taxing Economic Rents 1st Edition 2016. Taxing Economic Rents 2nd

Edition 2020.

<publisher Tim Walshaw>

<Canberra, Australia>

Email: timbot99@gmail.com

<2020>

Dedicated

to

Professor Arthur B. Laffer

Attributed to be the

discoverer of the so-called

Laffer Curve

Index

Introduction

What is the Laffer Curve? The Laffer Curve was first described, as far as it is known, by Professor Arthur Laffer in the 1970's. The Laffer Curve can be best described as an inverted 'U' drawn on a chart, where the 'y' axis is the total tax revenue, and the 'x' axis is the average tax rate. Conceptually then, tax revenue rises to a peak as the average tax rate rises, and then falls as the average tax rate increases. A further expansion of this hypothesis would be that the amount of tax revenue at each end of this curve starts at zero; the revenue at the left-hand curve starts at zero when the average tax rate starts at zero; and finally, the growth of revenue decelerates as average tax rate rises to its peak, and then after the peak the revenue falls at an accelerating rate until there is zero revenue at a certain tax rate.

The above theoretical statement cannot be disputed. Tax revenues must theoretically rise and then fall with the increase of the tax rate. Economists do not dispute the theory, or the possibility of a Laffer Curve. Some, many, just dispute its practical existence.

A chart of a Laffer Curve is shown below:

Diagram 1

The Laffer Curve

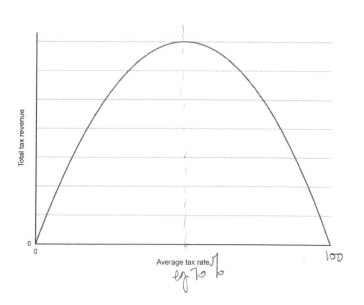

Can the shape and position of the Laffer Curve be measured? In this book, a method to do this is described. Then figures are attached to this estimated Laffer Curve. From that policy recommendations are made.

This question is central to the question of the practical existence of the Laffer Curve, and from that, whether useful policy conclusions can be drawn. In this book, a method to measure the Laffer Curve is described; and using that methodology, data is used to derive a measure for the Laffer Curve in the USA. From that derived information, policy recommendations are made.

Chapter 1

Background

History is full of examples of nations and empires collapsing, a major reason being given by historians is excess taxation. Taxes rise, the economy collapses, there is social unrest, there is invasion and defeat, finitum. Given the central role of excess taxation in the history of economic collapse, I am amazed at the minimal attention that has been paid to this subject. My suspicion is that all or most of the commentators want increased tax expenditure on their pet program(s), whether building palaces, increasing the military, or increasing welfare; and ignore the consequences.

The only relationship that appears to relate increased taxation to falling revenue is the Laffer Curve. This curve relates increasing tax rates to rising, then falling, tax revenues. See the diagram below. The Laffer Curve was proposed at a luncheon in the early 1970's by Arthur Laffer, and popularized by Jude Wanniski (Wanniski, 1978). Laffer proposed a diagram with two axes. The vertical axis is taxation revenue and the horizontal axis is the average tax rate. The curve is an inverted 'u' with one leg placed

4

axiomatically at zero tax revenue and zero tax rate, and the other leg at an unspecified tax rate, where taxation revenue is again zero. At the center of the upturned 'u' there is a peak. To the left of the peak, revenue rises with the increasing tax rate, as most non-economists naturally expect. To the right of the peak, as the tax rate increases, revenue falls. Eventually at a certain tax rate, revenue falls to zero.

Diagram 2

The Laffer Curve

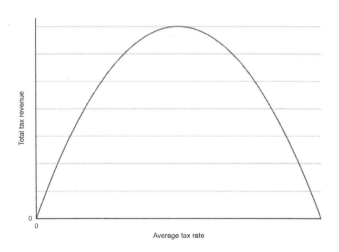

FIGURE 1. DIAGRAM OF THE LAFFER CURVE

As can be seen from the above chart, as the average tax rate rises, the rate of revenue increase fall; until the peak is reached where revenue does not increase as the tax rate rises. Then as the tax rate continues to rise, revenue fall, and falls at an increasing rate until at a certain average tax revenue falls to zero.

For most people not familiar with the Laffer Curve, while they may understand that revenue falls at an increasing rate, they cannot get their head around the fact, the certainty, that revenue will fall as the tax rate continues to rise. They get offended, especially as the ruler, tax adviser, politician, has some pet expenditure project for which they want to raise further taxes. They do not want to think that there are some limits on their spending and taxing activities, beyond their political powers.

While there can be no objection among economists to the theoretical existence of the Laffer Curve, there have been many visceral objections among economists that it exists in practice. Estimates have been made of the peak of the Laffer Curve using various methodologies. These range from Y. Hsing (1986) who gives a revenue maximizing personal income tax rate of between 32.67 percent and 35.21 percent, ranging to 100 percent (J. Malcomson (1986)).

Hitherto there has been no method to estimate the shape of the Laffer Curve. There has been no theoretical explanation connecting the Laffer Curve with other taxation concepts such as Excess Burden of Taxation. In this book I attempt to do so.

Chapter 2

The Excess Burden of Taxation

In this book, I derive the Laffer Curve theoretically from the concept of the Excess Burden of Taxation. However, it is first necessary to describe the Excess Burden of Taxation.

A. Definition of Excess burden

"Loss of economic activity due to the imposition of a tax compared to a free market with no tax." Farlex Financial Dictionary, 2012, Farlex Inc.

B. Theory of Excess Burden

The theory of Excess Burden goes back to Hicks, but the two current major authorities are Auerbach and Hines (2001) and Feldstein (2008), who have each written many papers on this subject.

So, what is Excess Burden, otherwise known in the literature as the Deadweight Loss?

Diagram 3

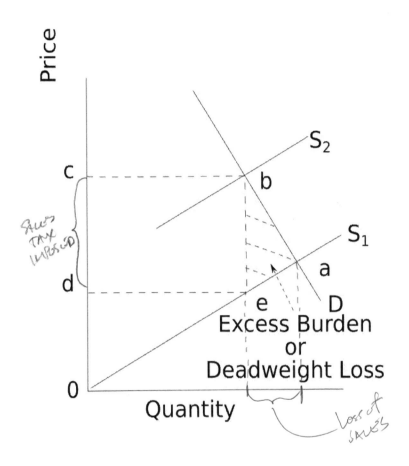

DIAGRAM 2. EXPLANATORY DIAGRAM OF
THE CAUSE OF EXCESS BURDEN

I turn to the standard supply/demand diagram above of the imposition of a tax. D is the demand line and S_1 and S_2 are the supply lines, moving from S_1 to S_2 as a consequence of the imposition of an ad-valorem tax value eb. In this diagram, to the right of the line eb, made by dropping a line from the intersection of the second supply line and the demand line, is a triangle made by the demand line, the first supply line and the line eb.

What is the meaning of this triangle? This triangle describes an area of invisible loss caused by imposing the tax. The value of the tax imposed is the area bcde. However the loss to the taxpayer caused by the shift of the supply line upwards is the area bcdea. This loss is over and above the amount of the tax value bcde. This loss was traditionally known in economic analysis as the 'deadweight loss', but in taxation analysis it has come to be called 'excess burden of taxation', a term initially coined by Harberger (1971), and this area is often called the 'Harberger triangle'

So what is happening in the above diagram?

In this example a sales tax is imposed, at an amount eb. This has the effect of moving the Supply line up from S1 to S2, as the cost is increased. The tax causes the loss triangle eba.

As can be seen from the above triangle, these losses are not negligible. In this diagram it is about 20 per cent of the total tax paid.

10

This Excess Burden is a hidden loss to the economy. It cannot be directly measured in terms of tax dollars, but there are methodologies available which can indirectly estimate this amount. But, even though the Excess Burden loss appears "theoretical" it has a very real loss on the economy, and this amount can be estimated.

Its effect is just like the tax imposed by an enemy power, it is money and resources taken from the economy and it is not returned. Unlike most taxation, Excess Burden is a net loss to the economy. Thus, the effect of Excess Burden is far more serious than any other tax imposed on the economy, as most taxes are normally paid back into the economy.

Chapter 3

Deriving the Laffer Curve from a measure of Excess Burden

To do this we create a simple economic model. In this model I make certain assumptions.

The basic assumption is that at a zero tax rate, zero tax revenue is raised. This ties one leg of the Laffer Curve to zero on both axes.

The next assumption is that total economic activity is related to the net profit less the "real" tax – defined as the actual tax plus the excess burden.

Where net profit is zero, total economic activity is zero, and the total revenue is zero. (It is noted in the economic literature; some economists oppose this salient point. Some say that the economy will continue to operate when there is zero revenue due to excess burden, as there will be tax avoidance, or the populace will resort to barter!).

The above concept ties the next leg of the Laffer Curve to the place where net profit is zero, the point where actual tax plus the excess burden takes 100 percent of profit.

Thus, the Laffer Curve is tied to two points on the 'x' axis where tax revenue is zero.

The question is – is the curve in between an inverted 'u' with a maximum with positive revenue, and declining revenue past the maximum point?

We can first work out the theoretical structure of the Laffer Curve, and then with the parameter for the excess burden curve already we can we can put figures to the point where the maximum is.

Definitions

A   Business activity

P   Profit

T   Tax rate

E   Excess burden

L   The "real" tax rate $= T + E$

R   Tax revenue

Find R in terms of T.

Assume business activity A is a function of net profit.

Net profit is total Profit P less the real rate of tax $T + E$ (not just T as Excess Burden affects total Profit P, even though it cannot be seen. I refer back to the initial supply/demand diagram. Excess Burden affects both Supply and Demand, causing loss to both the supplier and the consumer).

We assume that the initial profit P is constant and is not affected by the tax rate, and is a maximum when tax and excess burden is zero. Also assume a linear relationship between business activity and net profit.

Thus

(1) $\qquad A = \text{fn} (P - L)$

or

(2) $\qquad A = n (P - L)$ where n is a parameter constant

Tax revenue R is equal to business activity A times the tax rate T.

Thus

(3) $R = A \times T$

Thus to find tax revenue R in terms of tax rate T, substitute in (2) to eliminate A.

Then

(4) $R = n(P - L) \, T$

Substitute $L = T + E$ to eliminate L

(5) $R = n \, (P - (T + E)) \, T$

Now it is necessary to normalize these variables to become ratios of the Tax Base B. Divide by B.

Then $R?$

(6) $r = R/B$ $P?$

(7) $p = P/B$ $T?$

(8) $t = T/B$ $E?$

(9) $e = E/B$

Thus, the insert into the above formula (5) the variables reduced to ratios of the tax base B

(10) $r = n(p - (t - e))t$

John Creedy (2004) and Ballard, Fullerton, Shoven and Whalley (1985) have shown that rate of deadweight losses approximately increase with the square of the tax rate. and linearly with elasticities.

To be more precise I shall quote the function derived by Creedy (2004) page 17.

(11) $$EB_{cv} = (|\eta_0|/2)\,(X_0 P_0)\,t^2$$

where

EB_{cv} is rate of excess burden s

η_0 is the Hicksian point elasticity of demand

Creedy's methodology assumes a horizontal supply curve. However as point elasticities are assumed a cross elasticity of supply and demand would be constant.

X_0 is the initial quantity of goods or activity

P_0 is the initial price

(the product of these is called initial income)

t is the rate of tax

Thus, the level of excess burden is a function of the level of the rate of tax squared, keeping elasticity constant.

To keep things simple in this derivation I assume that the elasticity remains constant. I have taken the average tax rate to be the total tax revenue divided by the tax base.

It is more frequent to compare tax revenue to GDP. The proportion of tax to GDP in the US was 26.9 percent in 2014 (source Bureau of Economic Analysis (BEA)).

However, in the formulation used here the tax is related to taxable income (the tax base). GDP includes government tax revenue. Let taxable income (the potential total tax base) be GDP less government tax revenue.

Thus t, the average rate of tax = government tax revenue/tax base

= (government tax revenue)/ (GDP – government tax revenue)

where GDP – government tax revenue = the tax base.

Given the relationship between the average tax rate and excess burden, excess burden losses increase with the square of the tax rate, the relation of the tax rate T to the excess burden can be described in a formula

(12) $$e = fn\ t^2$$

or $e = at^2$ assuming the relationship is linear, as the elasticity η_0 in the above function $EB_{cv} = (|\eta_0|/2)\ (X_0 P_0)\ t^2$ is a point elasticity, and $X_0 P_0$ is constant.

e = EB$_{cv}$ is the percentage of the Excess Burden to the tax base and t is the average tax rate percent.

e = at^2 is the formula of a parabola going through the position (0,0).

This formula can be used to derive the Laffer Curve, going through a number of simple intermediate steps.

Now

(13) $e = at^2$

Substitute for e in formula (10)

(14) $r = n (p - (t + at^2)) t$

Expanding

(15) $r = n (pt - t^2 - at^3)$

This is the formula of the Laffer Curve. It is a cubic curve, commencing at the intersection r = 0 and t = 0.

t, the tax rate, is a positive value, and lies between 0 and 1. The curve goes through (0,0). It also goes through a second point where r =0 where $(pt - t^2 - at^3) = 0$.

As the curve is cubic it has a maximum and a minimum. As the maximum of the curve lies between the points t = 0 and $(pt - t^2 - at^3) = 0$ the curve is concave between those two points.

The maximum point of the Laffer Curve $2t + 3at^2 = p$ shows that t, the maximum tax ratio of the Laffer Curve, is dependent on the profit rate p. In periods when the profit rate is high, t increases, and thus maximum point of the Laffer Curve moves to the right. When the profit rate is lower, the maximum of the Laffer Curve moves to the left. Therefore, it is incumbent on any government, if it desires to increase its maximum possible tax rate, to take steps to increase the pre-tax profit rate.

The amount of profit P in the economy is the conceptual remainder of the value of Labor to Output in the economy. There has been controversy that the ratio of the value of profits to labor has expanded over recent years. The increase in the proportion of P has pushed the peak of the Laffer Curve to the right. If this proportion reverses, the peak of the Laffer Curve will move to the left. As tax revenue has almost reached the Laffer Curve peak, any reversal of the Profit/Labor proportion is likely to lead to a fall in revenue as the tax ratio is now on the right side of the pcak of the Laffer Curve.

Chapter 4

The cost of Excess Burden

Now these Excess Burden losses are not, as I said, something theoretical and do not exist. These losses exist and can be measured. They depend of course on the elasticities of supply and demand (Feldstein (2008)).

So what are these losses? Have they been measured?

At this point I will say that two types of deadweight losses can be measured, the average deadweight loss, which is the size of the above triangle, and the marginal deadweight loss, which is a measure of the incremental change of the average deadweight loss as the tax value changes.

For simplicity I shall stick to average deadweight loss. Suffice to say marginal deadweight losses have been measured as two to three times the average deadweight losses, so there is no respite from this analysis by going in that direction.

A useful summary of the measures of average deadweight losses is in the CIS Report "Cost of Taxation", (Robson 2005) Robson provides a couple of useful tables. These are:

TABLE 1 - US ESTIMATES OF THE AVERAGE
DEADWEIGHT COSTS OF ALL TAXES

Study	Estimate percentage of the tax
Ballard et al (1985)	23.8
Jorgenson and Yun (1990)	21.2
Jorgenson and Jun (1991)	18

Now this value of excess burden only relates to the tax rates prevalent at the time - 1990.

These measured values of the excess burden are not insignificant. We are just talking here about the "Economic cost", not the Administrative and Compliance costs.

All these measures are for the United States. My searches have found no empirical results of excess burden anywhere outside the United States, or since that date in the United States. Like all things, fashions come and go, and when the specialists in this area retired, no-one stepped up to take their place.

Chapter 5

The process of estimating the values of the Laffer Curve

Step 1. Deriving the value of the parameter a.

I use the latest excess burden figure is the one derived by Jorgenson and Yu in 1991. This is 18 percent.

I shall use the US statistics published by the Bureau of Economic Analysis (BEA). I shall use the statistics for the year 1990, which I assume was the set of statistics used by Jorgenson and Yu.

So first of all, what is the Tax Ratio?

It is easy enough to choose the Tax Ratio as the ratio of total government tax revenue to GDP. However Jorgenson and Yu did not use GDP in their estimate of the Excess Burden percent. They used non-government income.

This figure can be estimated by deducting Government Tax Revenue from GDP. This gives the Government Revenue Tax Base. (Obviously the government does not tax itself).

So:

GDP of the USA in 1990 was $5979.6 billion in current dollars. (Source BEA GDP spreadsheet).

Total government tax revenue in 1990 = $1712.9 billion. (Source BEA Tax Revenue spreadsheet).

Total tax base in 1990 = $5979.6 - $1712.9 billion

$$= \$4263.7 \text{ billion}$$

Tax ratio t   = Tax Receipts/Tax Base

$$= 1712.9/4263.7$$

t $= 0.401740$ or 40.17 percent

Now   e $= at^2$

a $= e/t^2$

a $= 18/(40.17)^2$

a $= 0.01115274$

This parameter is used throughout this successive work to find the Laffer Curve.

Step 2. Estimating the curve relating the value of the Excess Burden to the Tax Ratio

This step is optional, but the curve is interesting as it illustrates the rapid increase in excess burden with the increasing tax rate.

The values for e and t have been calculated in the following table using the formula $e = at^2$ and substituting for a = 0.01115274.

TABLE 2 - THE VALUE OF THE AVERAGE TAX RATIO t TO THE EXCESS BURDEN RATIO e

t	e
Percent	Percent
0	0
5	0.28
10	1.12
15	2.51
20	4.46
25	6.98
30	10.03
35	13.66
40	17.84
45	22.58
50	27.88
55	33.73

60	40.15
70	54.65
80	71.38

Diagram 5

Chart of the above table

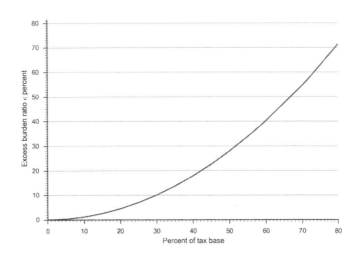

FIGURE 3. THE RELATIONSHIP BETWEEN THE
PROPORTION OF EXCESS BURDEN AND THE TAX
RATIO

e is the rate of the Excess Burden percent of tax base

t is rate of taxation percent of tax base

Rate of taxation percent of tax base is a proxy for the average tax rate.

While these results may be rough and ready they demonstrate two essential points. First, the present tax to GDP ratio in the USA is around 27 percent. This gives the percentage tax to tax base ratio of around 36 percent, giving a current excess burden around 14 percent from the above table.

The second point is that this excess burden is increasing at a rapid rate as the average tax rate rises, as can be seen in the above chart.

Step 3. What is the total tax rate, defined as the average tax rate plus the excess burden?

The question arises at what point does the total of the actual tax plus the corresponding excess burden equals 100 percent? That is, at what point does the actual tax plus the hidden tax of excess burden take everything? This is a question taxation economists have never really asked.

The actual tax rate plus the rate of excess burden is summed in the table below

TABLE 3 – TABLE OF AVERAGE TAX RATE t, EXCESS BURDEN e AND SUM OF BOTH t + e

Average Tax Rate t	Excess Burden ratio e	Sum of t + e
Percent	Percent	Percent
0	0	0
5	0.28	5.28
10	1.11	11.11
15	2.51	17.51
20	4.46	24.46
25	6.97	31.97
30	10.04	40.04
35	13.66	48.66
40	17.84	57.84
45	22.58	67.58
50	27.88	77.88

55	33.74	88.74
60	40.15	100.15

Diagram 6

Chart of the above table

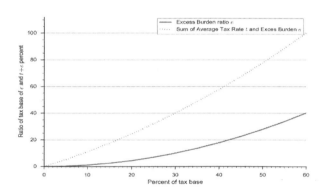

FIGURE 4. ADDING THE RATE OF EXCESS
BURDEN TO THE AVERAGE TAX RATE.

As can be seen from the position of the dotted line at the
100 percent total of the Excess Burden and the actual tax
rate, a tax rate of 60 percent leads to a total confiscation of
all income as excess burden takes the balance.

Is this a point of total catastrophe?

Maybe a case can be made that the non-excess burden component taxation is spent again in the economy, a 60 percent tax rate is not a point of total collapse. Nevertheless at this tax rate there is an invisible tax rate of 40 percent, the excess burden, which is not returned to the economy. It is equivalent to a foreign invader imposing a tax of 40 percent and taking it all out of the country. It is difficult to argue that at a 60 percent tax rate the country is at the very least severely debilitated, if only as the consequence of the 40 percent excess burden.

Step 4. Deriving the Laffer Curve values

Now we can put some figures on this curve.

We know that a = 0.0115274.

We assume that the initial profit rate P is constant and does not change as the tax rate rises.

Since r and t are measured in percentage terms, let p, the initial profit rate when tax is zero, be 100 percent.

$$r = n \, (pt - t^2 - at^3)$$

Let n be 1 for this exercise. To be precise the value of n $= (|\eta_0|/2) \, (X_0 P_0)$,

where η_0 is the point elastictity at the point $X_0 P_0$. Whatever its real value, its only effect would be to move the

31

curve up and down in the vertical direction, not left and right. It will not affect the shape of the Laffer Curve or the position of the peak.

Thus $r = (1t - t^2 - 0.0011527\, t^3)$.

Estimating r for t from 0 to 1.0 (100 percent) we get the following results:-

TABLE 4 – TAX REVENUE r IN TERMS OF AVERAGE TAX RATE t

Tax Rate t	Tax Revenue r
Percent	(measured as percent of maximum profit)
0	0
5	4.8
10	9.0
15	12.7
20	16.0
25	18.7
30	21.0
35	22.7
40	23.9

45	24.6
50	24.8
55	24.5
60	23.7
65	22.3
70	20.4
75	18.0
80	15.1
85	11.7
90	7.8
95	3.3
99	0.0

The calculated Laffer Curve is below.

Diagram 7

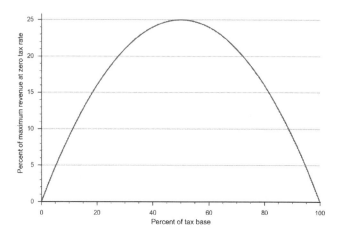

FIGURE 5. THE VALUES OF THE LAFFER
CURVE DERIVED BY USING THE MODEL AND THE
VALUE OF PARAMETER a

Note: The peak of this curve is slightly to the left of the
50 percent mark, and the curve reaches the "x" axis slightly
left of the 100 percent mark. The position and shape of the
Laffer Curve depends on the value of the parameter a. That
the maximum of this particular curve is in the region of the
50 percent average tax ratio and the far end reaches the "x"
axis near the 100 percent average tax ratio mark is probably
a coincidence, depending on economic conditions at the
time.

As can be seen, the maximum point on the Laffer Curve in the USA is around 50 percent average tax rate based on the tax revenue to potential tax base. This works out as 33 percent of the tax to GDP ratio.

Since the average tax rate in the USA is around 27 percent of GDP, the lesson from this is that the USA has nearly reached the peak of the Laffer Curve. Any further increases in the tax rate will lead to constant tax revenue and then falling tax revenue. Total revenue will plateau and then start falling, and at a faster and faster rate until the average tax rate reaches 60 percent, (about 40 percent of tax to GDP ratio) when the total tax take including excess burden is 100 percent. The USA has about reached its limits in taxation.

Chapter 6

Other countries' Laffer Curves

As far as I could find, excess burden figures have not been published for any country outside the United States, so at the moment no Laffer Curves can be estimated for them. It is a matter of surmise whether these countries have the same shaped Laffer Curve as the United States with a peak average tax rate to tax base of 50 percent or a tax rate to GDP ratio of 33 percent.

A look at a list of the ratios of tax to GDP of various countries provided shows that many countries have passed this 33 percent ratio mark.

The following is a selection of six countries in the EU that have ratios of tax collected to GDP over 40 percent. (Source: Eurostat. Total Tax Revenue by Country 1995-2014 (percent of GDP). Total receipts from taxes and social contributions (incl. imputed social contributions) after deduction of amounts assessed but unlikely to be collected percent).

TABLE 5 – TOP SIX COUNTRIES IN THE EU IN TERMS OF PERCENT OF TAX TO GDP

Country	2009 percent of tax to GDP	2014 percent of tax to GDP
Denmark	46.5	50.8
Belgium	45.2	47.8
France	43.9	47.9
Finland	41.1	44.0
Austria	42.0	43.7
Italy	42.0	43.7

A striking feature of this table is that not only are these percentages well above the 30 percent mark of the described Laffer Curve, but in those six years the tax rate has increased significantly.

The following is a table describing the actual revenue raised in each of those countries between 2009 and 2014.

38

(Eurostat. Total tax revenue by country 1995-2014 (millions of Euro). Total receipt from taxes and social contributions after deductions assessed but unlikely to be collected in millions of Euro).

TABLE 6 – TOP SIX COUNTRIES IN THE EU IN
TERMS OF TOTAL TAX REVENUE COLLECTED IN
SIX CONSECUTIVE YEARS 2009 – 2014 IN MILLIONS
OF EUROS

Count ry	2 009	2 010	2 011	2 012	2 013	2 014
Denm ark	974, 306	986, 534	1,045, 641	1,082, 636	1,111, 280	1,151, 482
Belgi um	157, 492	166, 116	174,9 88	183,2 85	189,3 90	191,9 30
Franc e	851, 105	880, 584	931,1 69	979,2 71	1,002, 349	1,021, 116
Finla nd	74,3 23	76,5 69	80,01 1	85,53 6	88,95 8	90,25 3
Austri a	101, 585	115, 739	123,4 38	127,4 97	129,7 38	135,5 34
Italy	660, 244	669, 845	638,5 29	705,3 15	700,9 04	704,9 01

If these countries have approximately the same peak of
the Laffer Curve as the United States, as their rate of tax is

40

well of this peak rate of 33 percent in the years 2009 and 2014, one would expect their tax revenues over these years to fall. As shown by the above table the tax revenues show no sign of doing this. Both the rates and the revenues over these six years have climbed hardly without interruption.

The interpretation of this result is that either there is something seriously wrong with the theory, or the Laffer Curve peaks for these countries are much higher than for the United States, or something is going on that allows these countries to continue to raise revenue well past their Laffer Curve peaks.

As the development of the theory appears to be logical, and appears to be based on sound theory, other reasons for the continued growth in tax revenue have to be carefully looked at.

I do not have available figures for the average excess burden of taxation for these countries, so I have not been able to estimate the peaks of their respective Laffer Curve. However, I feel that while there could be some divergence in these values of each of these countries and the United States, I do not feel that these divergences could have allowed the above results. One would expect that tax revenues would be falling when they reached well below the percentage rates reported.

So, what else could be happening?

1. The Laffer curve peak for each of these countries could be much higher. As I do not have the excess burden figures for each of these countries I am unable to test this.

2. As is happening at present, governments are substituting borrowing and money printing for raising tax revenue. Given this stimulus, these governments may be able to raise the tax rate to higher levels than the peak of the Laffer Curve with no accompanying fall in tax revenue. A following question is, for how long can this borrowing and money printing policy be sustained? If this policy ceases to be viable and effective and the country has to resort to raising revenue by taxation only, there will be a dramatic fall in revenue as taxation revenue returns to the peak of the Laffer Curve regardless of the tax rates.

3. An alternative explanation is that the measures of GDP for these European countries is around 30 percent below similar GDP measures in the United States. The reason for this explanation is that if the same conversion rate between the tax to GDP ratio and the tax to tax-base rate is used as in the United States, the tax to tax-base ratio for the country with a 50.8 percent tax to GDP ratio would be around 77 percent. This is unbelievable. Comparative methodologies between the US and European countries for calculating the GDP need careful checking.

4. The profit rates p, in the above formula, could be vastly higher in these countries. This allows them to push the peak of the Laffer Curve to the right.

5. The taxed economy in these countries could be split into different sectors. The business sector of the economy, especially the companies, could be taxed at a low rate, and the personal/employment tax sector could be taxed at a high rate.

   For personal employment the supply/demand elasticities used to estimate excess burden could be inelastic. As a consequence (see the supply/demand diagram at the beginning of this article) the excess burden in this sector would be very low. As a consequence the peak of the Laffer Curve for the personal employment tax sector could be very much higher than 33 percent. Higher taxes could be raised from this personal employment sector without a fall in revenue.

   To test this hypothesis it would be necessary to show two things:

   i. The proportion of taxes raised from the business sector, especially the corporate sector is low, and

   ii. The relevant supply/demand elasticities used to estimate the excess burden for personal employment are more elastic than for the business sector.

6.   Total taxation, as has already been described, has two parts, the actual taxation and excess burden. Excess burden tax just disappears, and is a drag on the economy. On the other hand, the actual tax revenue levied is normally spent in the economy. It is not a total loss to the economy. Some tax expenditure has a multiplier effect, and generates benefits to the economy and cause it to grow. Other tax expenditures have a negative multiplier. Thus depending on the structure of tax expenditure, if these countries have the same Laffer curve as the US, even though the tax rate has exceeded 45 percent (and the total tax rate has reached 100 percent), it is possible that as some or most of the actual tax revenue is re-circulated through the economy, harm is minimized. Thus it may look as if governments can continue to raise increasing levels of taxation to quite high levels without causing a total collapse of the economy, as would be expected if the actual tax rate plus the excess burden at that rate exceeds 100 percent.

Chapter 7

Macroeconomic questions

I have not attempted to go into the macroeconomic question whether a cut in the average tax rate below 27 percent will increase growth and thereby increase revenue that way. There was some experience under President Reagan that this is what happened, to the continued surprise of many economists. This is an explanation. The tax cut carried with it a cut in a nearly equal hidden tax, the Excess Burden. This was in effect a "double whammy", and highly beneficial for the economy. It is sufficient to say in this paper that increasing taxes in the USA from the just above the present level will certainly decrease tax revenue.

All the taxes in the USA, and indeed the rest of the world, are beset by the effects of Excess Burden. The only taxes that do not have Excess Burden are taxes with vertical supply lines such as land taxes or lump sum taxes of various sorts. Also, taxes on economic rents do not have Excess Burden effects. (However, taxes with zero Excess Burden, if they are not taxes on economic rents they do have a Laffer Curve, but the peak is much higher). For those without the immediate knowledge of economic theory in this area, and are somewhat dumbfounded by this statement, I suggest reading my book "Taxing Economic Rents". This has a clear exposition of the theory and the issues involved. The Second Edition is a bit more technical, and covers taxing lenders and banks.

Chapter 8

The Laffer Curve for Government Expenditure

If there is a Laffer curve for taxation, it could be inferred that there is a Laffer Curve for government expenditure. The expansionary effect of increasing government expenditure could have decreasing returns, zero returns, and then negative returns, just in the Laffer Curve for taxation previously described. Increasing government expenditure could actually decrease economic growth.

An initial question is, what would be the axes of this Laffer Curve?

An obvious pair would be Change in Government Expenditure on the 'y' axis, and Change in Private Expenditure on the 'x' axis.

Data was obtained from the Australian National Accounts Statistics, ABS 5206.0, National Income, Expenditure and Product, June 2019, Table 3, Expenditure on Gross Domestic Product (GDP) Current Prices, General Government – Final Consumption Expenditure A22298AT from September Quarter 1959. 159 quarters of data.

In this experiment, quarterly data was chosen. If the size of the government expenditure is denoted as G, the change in government expenditure in a particular quarter is denoted as $\Delta G_n = G_n \,/\, G_{n-1}$.

Similarly, if private expenditure is denoted as P, , the change in private expenditure in a particular quarter is denoted as $\Delta P_n = P_n \,/\, P_{n-1}$.

The chart is below.

Diagram 8

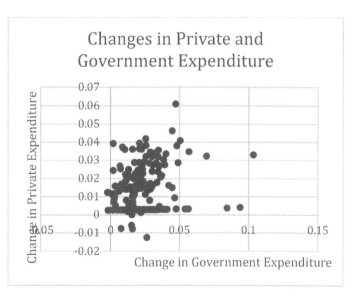

The change in government expenditure is absolute change, not in percentage terms. Thus 0.04 in an increase of four per cent per quarter.

As can be seen, the results are from first sight meaningless. There appears to be little relationship between changes in Government Expenditure and changes in Private Expenditure. The many researchers and students who have tried this no doubt got discouraged, as, while Government Expenditure sometimes appears to have some effect on Private Expenditure, sometimes it has no effect, and there is definitely no direct and stable relationship.

But what about an underlying cause and effect? What about the multiplier?

The size of the multiplier in that quarter is denoted as M_n. The size of the fiscal multiplier for the purpose of this experiment is equal to the change in private ec

Private economic activity in the same quarter, denoted as ΔP_n, divided by the change in government expenditure in that quarter, ΔG_n.

Or

$M_n = \Delta P_n\ /\ \Delta G_n$

The data used was From the Australian National Accounts Statistics, ABS 5206.0, National Income, Expenditure and Product, June 2019, Table 3, Expenditure on Gross Domestic Product (GDP) Current Prices, General Government – Final Consumption Expenditure A22298AT from September Quarter 1959. 159 quarters of data.

The chart below shows the results.

Diagram 9

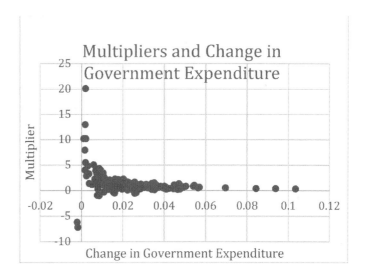

As can be seen, the points follow a curve that closely follows the left-hand axis to a certain point, then turns a corner, and closely follows the 'y'axis. The curve is concave towards the origin.

This is a far more meaningful result, and it implies that the underlying Expenditure Laffer Curve relates to the relationship between the Private Expenditure Multiplier and the Change in Government Expenditure. The reason for this is clear. The influence of changes in Government expenditure on changes in Private Expenditure depends on the direct relationship between the size of those changes., as in the multiplier. The size of the changes themselves are insufficiently close.

I considered fitting a curve towards these points and taking the values, but then the argument would be sidelined towards the values of the curve.

In general terms, the implications of the shape of this curve is clear. There are major decreasing returns between changes in Government Expenditure and the Multiplier. High values of the Multiplier only occur when the increase in Government expenditure is very small. Indeed, in this chart, Multipliers with values in excess of 2.5 only occur if the increase in Government Expenditure is less than 0.01, or 1 per cent per quarter. If the increases in Government Expenditure exceed 1 per cent per quarter, this has no effect to increase the Multiplier.

The Government Expenditure Laffer Curve

While a fitted curve appears to closely follow the 'y' axis, theoretically the curve must turn and go through the 'x' axis. Why? There is a point when any increase in Government Expenditure has zero effect. At this point there is a level of "natural" growth in Private Income, not stimulated by government expenditure. Alternatively, if all private growth needs to be stimulated increases in

Government Expenditure, this line must go through the origin.

Conceptually therefore, the chart follows the following shape. The chart shape is skewed so that the mode is moved towards the 'y' or Change in Private Income axis.

Diagram 10

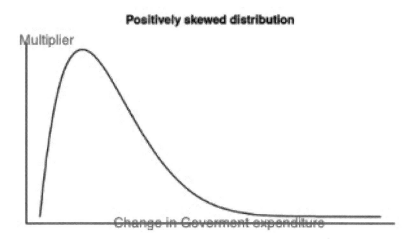

The results closely reflect the more skewed line in the above diagram. Why? Because the left-hand points closely follow the 'y' axis. But it is not clear which points are on the line "on the way up" or which points are on the line 'on the way down'.

So finally, a Government Expenditure Laffer Curve exists, with the 'y' axis being the values of the Multiplier, and the 'x' axis being the change in Government Expenditure. The peak is hardly detectable as the curve is highly skewed.

Virtually any increase in government expenditure leads to decreasing levels of multiplier effectiveness. The multiplier falls as the level of government expenditure increases.

A diagram of the curve of the Government Expenditure Laffer curve is shown below.

Diagram 11

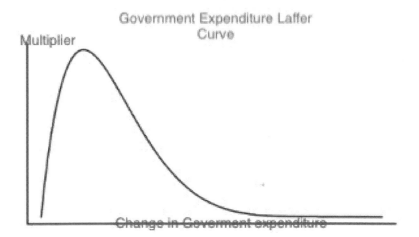

Government Expenditure Laffer Curve

Conclusion

The Laffer Curve was derived in this book from the concept of Excess Burden. John Creedy (2004) and Ballard, Fullerton, Shoven and Whalley (1985) have shown that rate of deadweight losses increase with the square of the tax rate and linearly with elasticities. A parameter can be derived connecting this relationship. A formulation can then be derived of the Laffer Curve utilizing this parameter.

This formulation can be used to plot part of a cubic curve on a chart with the vertical axis as tax revenue and the horizontal axis as the average tax rate. The cubic curve goes through (0.0), reaches a peak, then falls back to the zero tax revenue level.

Using the value of average Excess Burden estimated in 1991 (the latest available figure) and an estimated tax ratio for 1990, a parameter of the relationship between the excess burden and the square of the average tax ratio was estimated. This was inserted into the derived function of the Laffer Curve. This Laffer Curve was shown to have a peak of around 33 percent of the tax to GDP ratio in 1990.

The tax to GDP ratio in the USA is currently (2015) around 27 percent. If the Laffer Curve has remained the same since 1991, then the tax ratio is approaching the peak of the Laffer Curve.

This result indicates that pretty soon tax revenues in the United States will stabilize and then start falling regardless how much the tax ratio is raised. Increasing the tax rate will causes a fall in tax revenue from the peak of the Laffer Curve onwards. The government cannot rely on growth to increase tax revenue, as part of the reason the Laffer Curve declines is that growth becomes negative after the tax ratio passes the peak of the curve.

Government assumptions and beliefs regarding the possibility of increasing expenditure will have to change when the peak of the Laffer Curve is approached. Increasing the rate of tax or imposing new taxes will not necessarily increase revenue.

As a consequence, near the peak of the Laffer Curve, if government expenditure increases in one area, there must be a compensating reduction in expenditure in other areas, unless this increased expenditure is met by increased borrowing. As tax revenue is capped by outside economic forces at the peak of the Laffer Curve, this will impose a cap on tax expenditure. Even increased growth cannot be depended on, because as you raise the tax past the peak of the Laffer Curve the economy will stagnate and then decline.

As growth will be zero at the peak of the Laffer Curve an inference of this result is that, as you move down the left side of the Laffer Curve as the tax ratio decreases, growth increases. Lower tax leads to higher growth.

I suggest that an econometric model of the form $r = a + bt + ct^2 + dt^3$ be run, where r is tax revenue and t the tax ratio (not in percentage terms), and a, b, c and d are estimated parameters. I predict that a will be significantly no different from zero, and b and c are significantly no different from -1, whether t is the ratio of tax revenue to GDP or the tax base. The parameter d can be used to estimate the peaks of the Laffer Curve. Furthermore d can be used to estimate the average Excess Burden in the economy, that will match the values estimated by alternative methods.

Refinements of this methodology may be needed. What is also greatly needed is an updated value the current peak of the Laffer Curve for every country, derived from updated values of the Excess Burden in those countries.

Finally, I raise the question, is there a Laffer Curve for total government revenue? Theoretically, this should be the case.

The way that this was investigated was to look at the relationship between single period multipliers and the same period's increase in government expenditure. The single period multiplier chosen was the change in private expenditure divided by the change in government expenditure in the same period. In this investigation some 250 data points were estimated.

The results obtained were charted. The results appeared to be very interesting – a curve that appeared to be asymptotic to either axis, and curved towards the axis.

Thus, the Expenditure Laffer Curve is highly skewed, with the mode close to the 'x' axis. Thus, there would be little or no increasing returns relationship between a change in on Total Government Expenditure and a change in Private Expenditure. There would be a decreasing relationship over almost the entire curve, unlike a normal Laffer Curve.

In most empirical analyses to date, the only attempts that have been made is to estimate the "average" multiplier for a certain set of data such as a range of increases of government expenditure. Despite attempts at increasing refinement, the results have been highly variable. As far as I know, there have been no attempts to estimate a large number of multipliers for many different time periods. When this is done, as in the above, it will be seen that multipliers are wildly different according to the time period and the circumstances. There is no such thing as an "average".

For the original Laffer Curve, there are other sources of revenue beside taxes such as borrowing, printing money, duties on exports, sales of assets, and in the case of some, receipt of foreign aid. These revenues are an overlay on the

Laffer Curve that only reflects tax revenue. Is there a limit on the receipt of all of these, and will the "total revenue curve" turns down eventually as receipts dry up? Conceptually this is likely, but is there an economic rationale for this eventual total revenue down-turn? Can the total revenue peak be estimated?

So, in conclusion, the Laffer Curve exists. Both theoretically, and in practice. This has very real implications for tax policy and economic growth. Indeed, it has further and deeper implications – the very continued existence of the nation. It is now known that there is a definite limit to taxation beyond control of governments.

REFERENCES

Auerbach, Alan J and James R. Hines. 2001. "Taxation of
   Economic Efficiency", NBER Working Paper 8181,
   National Bureau of Economic Research.

Ballard, Charles, John Shoven, and John Whalley. 1985.
   "General Equilibrium Computations of the Marginal
   Welfare Costs of Taxes in the United States", A. E. R.
   75: 128-138

Ballard, Charles, Don Fullerton, John Shoven, and John
   Whalley. 1985. "A General Equilibrium Model for Tax
   Policy Evaluation", The University of Chicago Press,
   Chicago.

Creedy, John. 2003 "The excess burden of taxation and why
   it (approximately) quadruples when the tax rate
   doubles". New Zealand Treasury Working Paper, 03/29.

Creedy, John. 2004 "The excess burden of taxation".
   Australian Economic Review, Vol (37) (4): 454-464.

Creedy, John. 2009. "Personal income taxation: from theory
   to policy" Australian Economic Review, 42, (4): 496-506.

Feldstein, Martin. 1999. "Tax Avoidance and the
   Deadweight Loss of the Income Tax", Review of
   Economics and Statistics 81:4: 674-680

Feldstein, Martin. 2008, "Effects of Taxation on Economic Behavior". National Bureau of Economic Research, NBER Working Paper 13754.

Harberger, Arnold. 1971. "Three Basic Postulates for Applied Welfare Economics: an Interpretive Essay", J. E.L, 9: 785-97.

Hsing, Yu. 1996. "Estimating the Laffer Curve and Policy Implications", Journal of Socio-Economics, 25(3): 395-402.

Malcolmson, James. 1986, "Some analytics of the Laffer curve", Journal of Public Economics, 29(3): 263-279.

Robson, Alex. 2005. "The Cost of Taxation", Centre of Independent Studies, CIS Policy Monograph 68.

Wanniski, Jude. 1978. "Taxes, Revenue and the Laffer Curve". The Public Interest: 3-16.

Yorgenson, Dale and Yun, Kun-Young. 1990. "Tax Reform and Economic Growth", Journal of Political Economy 98:5: 151-93

Yorgenson, Dale and Yun, Kun-Young. 1991. "The Excess Burden of Taxation in the United States", Journal of Accounting and Finance 6:4: 487-509